SUMMARY & ANALYSIS

OF

WINNERS TAKE ALL

The **ELITE CHARADE** *of*
CHANGING *the* **WORLD**

A GUIDE TO THE BOOK
BY ANAND GIRIDHARADAS

NOTE: This book is a summary and analysis and is meant as a companion to, not a replacement for, the original book.

Please follow this link to purchase a copy of the original book: https://amzn.to/2OADrjr

TABLE OF CONTENTS

CHAPTER 7: ALL THAT WORKS IN THE MODERN WORLD 36

EDITORIAL REVIEW 40

BACKGROUND ON AUTHOR... 43

END OF BOOK SUMMARY 46

SYNOPSIS

In his thought-provoking book *Winners Take All: The Elite Charade of Changing the World*, Anand Giridharadas explores the intricate business and lucrative business that is philanthropy. Whenever a tragedy or crisis occurs, for example, an earthquake, famine, or disease outbreak, global philanthropists rush in to provide aid. Companies move in to help with social causes as part of their attempt to bring about social change. But are the elite really interested in making the world a better place for everybody?

Giridharadas contends that despite all the advancements in technology and innovation, very few Americans are enjoying the benefits. There is a massive and ever-increasing discrepancy in the income between the rich and poor. The marginalized masses are beginning to feel that the system is stacked against them, and they know that it's the elite who are responsible. This is creating resentment between the haves and the have-nots, which explains the intense protests that define the meetings between the world and corporate leaders.

The book is structured in such a way that each chapter drives the key point home. Giridharadas interviews well-known personalities and reveals their true intentions when it comes to social change. If the rich are genuinely interested in changing the world, then they should reform the current system characterized by low-paying jobs and unfair trade practices. But the wealthy would rather give donations to poor communities instead of fixing the broken system. For them, it has to be a win-win situation. Changing the global system that has benefited them for so long is simply not an option.

CHAPTER 1:
BUT HOW IS THE WORLD CHANGED?

Giridharadas contends that there are many people who harbor idealistic tendencies, naively believing that they can change the world for the better. Yet most of these individuals come from privileged backgrounds where they are groomed to become successful in the business world. Though they sometimes try to make a difference, the existing institutions and structures make it difficult to break away from the existing charade.

These world changers are led to believe that the best way to bring social change is by starting a business venture. Therefore, they end up creating "social enterprises" that have little impact in taking down the powers that be. Over time, those seeking social change swallow the lie that the world can only get better through market-friendly methods.

Key Takeaway: Maintaining the status quo never brings any meaningful social reform.

According to Giridharadas, one of the prevailing messages in the mind of most college students is that meaningful social reforms can only be achieved by first serving the status quo. This is a fallacy, as shown by the example of Hilary Cohen. She is a student at Georgetown University, which is well known for idealistic leanings. Though she wants to pursue a course in business, she finally settles on philosophy after reading the works of Aristotle. She adopts the idea that the pursuit of wealth ultimately never brings satisfaction.

Cohen takes up the mantle of being an agent of positive change. She ends up working for big firms like Goldman Sachs, convincing herself that she has to learn about money to improve the lives of the less fortunate. However, she soon finds out that all these capitalistic organizations merely use economic inequality as a slogan to attract the best college talent. Once she becomes part of the corporate system, she realizes that the big market players aren't serious about bettering the lives of the masses.

Key Takeaway: Fancy models of change touted by the business world are ineffective.

When Cohen accepted a job at McKinsey, she thought she would be collaborating with some of the best minds in changing the world. However, she discovered that McKinsey thinkers espouse the idea that the free market is the only way to pursue social change, not politics or the law. In other words, those who benefit the most from the current inequality are the ones who should have the privilege of dictating what kind of reforms are undertaken. Cohen stays with the company despite her misgivings. She convinces herself that all she has to do is learn how the system works and then use that expertise to solve social problems. She soon realizes that the training people receive in the business world is totally useless in solving the problems of the world.

For example, McKinsey has a template that employees are supposed to use to generate solutions to problems. Cohen discovers that employees rarely use this toolkit because it doesn't even work. Employees simply use their own logic and intelligence to define a solution and then incorporate the solution into the template. Corporations and even President Obama's administration end up recruiting McKinsey consultants to come up with transformational strategies because nobody outside the company knows that the template is ineffective.

Key Takeaway: Those who work in the corporate system for too long stop seeing the harmful effects of their actions.

According to Giridharadas, when the government brings in private sector consultants and financiers to solve public problems, they end up doing more harm than good. For example, when Wall Street is asked to improve the American economy, the consultants try to enhance productivity by cutting down on all costs, especially labor. This leads to layoffs, automation, and offshoring.

Yet most of the people who implement these strategies are individuals who left college believing that they were going to make the world a better place for everyone. These self-proclaimed change makers rationalize their actions by saying, "Okay, we caused these problems, but we also know how to solve problems." Such attitudes of entitlement make Cohen lose faith in the ability of big corporations to bring about real change.

Key Takeaway: World changers are often trapped by the prestigious lifestyle.

Though Cohen felt uncomfortable by all the compromises she and her colleagues were making, she still enjoyed the lifestyle. The money was good and she had opportunities to hob-nob with powerful public figures. Even when she left McKinsey to work with the Obama Foundation, she still earned a salary from the consulting firm.

Giridharadas argues that many good people also get caught in the same trap. They believe that they can make a difference without exposing the rot in the system. This way, they can keep the lifestyle they have become accustomed to. However, deep down they silently wonder if there is a better way that they can change the world.

CHAPTER 2: WIN-WIN

Giridharadas paints a grim picture of how seemingly well-intentioned philanthropists try to improve the lives of the poor without really challenging the true causes of their poverty. Wealthy business entrepreneurs come up with technologies and strategies that they believe can make people's lives better. Unfortunately, these attempts are always tied into a profit-making motive. They only step in to "help" if they know that they too will gain financially in some way. For the poor to gain, the rich must gain even more. Giridharadas sees this as a win-win situation where the winners or elites "change things without having to change a thing."

Key Takeaway: Real change only occurs when you examine your role in the problem.

After traveling to Tanzania and seeing impoverished children walking for miles to get a meal, Stacey Asher decided to start a charity organization. As a former hedge fund employee married to a husband who works in finance, she sees herself in the perfect position to help. However, just like many of her fellow entrepreneurial do-gooders, she creates a company to help the needy but fails to examine her role in perpetuating poverty. Giridharadas argues that people like Stacey never ask themselves how the financial institutions they work for worsen the lives of the poor.

For example, hedge funds are very creative in dodging taxes. Yet this income would do a lot more when used as foreign aid in poor countries. Even as Stacey was establishing her techno-utopian and capitalistic charity organization, Standard Chartered bank was suing the Tanzanian government for a "dirty debt" that they claimed the government owed them. This is a common strategy that multinational financial institutions use to fleece billions of dollars from developing nations. If Stacey is sincere in changing the lives of poor African orphans, she should first challenge her comrades in the financial sector to stop this dubious practice. Then developing nations would have enough money to feed their own people. Unfortunately, these entrepreneurs never want to upset their friends in high places, so they fail to seek genuine systemic reform.

Key Takeaway: Corporations believe that giving is simply a way to make more profits.

Social change through the win-win approach is a tantalizing prospect for many businesspeople, thanks to Stephen Covey's 7 *Habits of Highly Effective People*. The fourth habit states that win-win solutions are mutually beneficial for all because life should be cooperative rather than competitive. Giridharadas explains that businesses began to set up social enterprises that reduced suffering but also ended up making huge profits in the process. As long as you do some good, then there's no problem benefiting from the misfortunes of others.

In fact, corporations are encouraged to view poor people as customers. Instead of seeing Syrian refugees as a suffering people in need of compassion, the World Bank encourages host countries to view them as an opportunity for cheap labor. This kind of market thinking pushes the narrative that giving can be extremely lucrative for those willing to step in and help. These helpers get to maintain their lavish lifestyles without feeling guilty about the suffering of those around them.

Key Takeaway: Solving your needs doesn't automatically solve the needs of others.

The world is full of inspired visionaries who claim to espouse collective action for the common good. This is evident in the way entrepreneurs create businesses based on their passions and expertise, assuming that the benefits will automatically spillover to the rest of the world. Giridharadas offers the example of Justin Rosenstein, a Silicon Valley innovator who helped create various technologies such as Gmail chat, Google Drive, and the Facebook "Like" button. As a young millionaire, Rosenstein decided to spend his money on philanthropic causes. Relying on the prevailing win-win approach, he decided to create Asana, a company that sold collaborative software.

Rosenstein's logic was simple: If he could create software that helps groups of people work together, then humanity would boost its productivity. And when productivity improves, the human condition also gets better. According to Giridharadas, such an initiative will never bring the social changes necessary.

"One of the central economic challenges now facing his country is the remarkable stagnation in wages for half of Americans despite the remarkable growth in productivity" (Giridharadas, Ch. 2).

At the end of the day, the average worker gets paid a pittance compared to the super-profits that such collaborative software earns the elites.

Key Takeaway: Silicon Valley entrepreneurs only support change-makers who massage their egos.

Giridharadas states that the entrepreneurial class has one implicit rule: they will only contribute to change if the problem is framed in a way that makes them feel good. This is what Emmett Carson, a social justice advocate, discovered when he began running the Silicon Valley Community Foundation. As a black man from a working-class family, he held a win-lose view of social justice. Throughout his career with various foundations, Carson never felt any opposition. However, in Silicon Valley, he was told to cease using the term "social justice" because it made Valley entrepreneurs feel bad about their wealth and privilege.

People in Silicon Valley see social justice as a way of taking from the rich to give to the poor. This kind of win-lose approach makes them feel uncomfortable because they don't want their complicity in structural inequality to be highlighted. Ultimately, Carson was forced to change his stance from social justice to one of social fairness. By appeasing his philanthrocapitalist benefactors, he was able to continue receiving their generous donations.

CHAPTER 3:
REBEL-KINGS IN WORRISOME BERETS

One of the things about Silicon Valley entrepreneurs who wish to change the world is that they see themselves as rebels who are fighting against government control. Giridharadas contends that these privileged individuals see their businesses as a solution for mankind's problems. They forget that as barons of technology, they have built such a large fortune at the expense of the masses they claim to be serving. At the end of the day, what is needed is not an app or software. There has to be a transformation in everyone's mindset so that the economy is guided by mutualism and *cooperativism*.

Key Takeaway: Technology has widened the inequality gap.

Giridharadas describes how Silicon Valley entrepreneurs and financiers regularly meet to talk about how they are improving the lives of people. In these conferences, entrepreneurs from institutions like Apple, Google, PayPal, Uber, and Zappos claim that technology is the best way to bridge the gap between the rich and the poor. Yet as they enjoy the fruits of their labor, they fail to acknowledge the stark inequality that surrounds their daily lives.

According to Giridharadas, San Francisco, which is the home of Silicon Valley, is also the most unequal city in America. The average worker is finding it increasingly difficult to make a living because of the dismantling of the systems meant to protect the common man. The people responsible for dismantling the labor unions, job security laws, and zoning regulations are the wealthy technologists. Though they say that their businesses are changing the world, the elite are the only ones who are enjoying the benefits. Their actions are widening, not reducing, the inequality gap.

Key Takeaway: Technology barons push mankind in a specific direction by pretending to prophesize the future.

During the Mobile World Congress in Barcelona, Mark Zuckerberg stated that in a few years, most of the content consumed online would be in the form of video. Shervin Pishevar, the venture capitalist who funded Uber and Airbnb is quoted as saying that the future of civilization lies in life-extending technology. When powerful people like Zuckerberg and Pishevar say such things, they make everyone believe that they are merely thinkers or idealists who are predicting the future of mankind.

But Giridharadas argues that the elite are not prophesying the future—they are advocating for things they have already invested money in. Zuckerberg has the power to rewrite Facebook algorithms so that video posts become more common than text, thus earning him more advertising revenue. Pishevar is known to be pursuing life-extending technology for those who can afford to pay. So when

Silicon Valley barons claim to be describing some selfless idea, they are actually fighting for that specific thing to be accepted by everyone else. If they can convince everyone that their ideas occurred automatically rather than by design, people won't resent them for wielding such excessive power.

Key Takeaway: The elite see themselves as anti-establishment defenders of the truth.

During a Q-and-A session, Shervin Pishevar was asked how he would describe a world-changer. He stated that world-changers have "a willingness to fight for the truth…willing to take on power, no matter the cost." Pishevar then went on to describe how Uber was challenging "corrupt" government regulators and taxi unions who were opposing it. According to him, the existing structures of control were immoral and needed to be fought.

Giridharadas explains that these elite entrepreneurs view themselves as rebels fighting against the establishment. They are weak victims of excessive governmental control, and they must use technology to fight for their own version of the truth. However, they fail to realize that the same systems they are fighting against are the ones that protect the marginalized masses. They don't really care that their singular version of the truth is quite different from that of the common man.

The elites live out a fantasy of a world where there are no rules to be followed. This "Tyranny of Structurelessness" is meant to enable the powerful and strong to secede from popularly elected authorities. As Giridharadas puts it, this would allow "the Earl of Facebook and the Lord of Google to make major decisions about our shared fate outside of democracy."

Key Takeaway: The elites deny their moral responsibility to ensure justice.

Airbnb was engulfed in a racism storm when African Americans came out claiming that they were being denied housing due to their race. A black user proved this claim by creating a fake profile pretending to be a white guy. His accommodation request was immediately accepted. When complaints were made to the Department of Fair Employment and Housing, Airbnb claimed that it was simply a platform. Therefore, it had no moral duty to prevent racial discrimination by hosts, even though its own investigation showed there was clear racial bias.

According to Giridharadas, many Silicon Valley entrepreneurs refuse to accept that they have the power to make a difference. Many of them came up as hackers and renegades: outsiders who were powerless. But even after joining the powerful elite, they continue to deny their moral responsibility to ensure social justice. They sell technology as a means of addressing social problems.

However, they fail to exercise their power to make a genuine difference.

CHAPTER 4:
THE CRITIC AND THE THOUGHT LEADER

Giridharadas explores the differences between those who use their expertise to seek genuine change and those who are interested in pandering to the elites. Both nationally and globally, critics of structural inequality are pushed aside because their ideas are radical and don't fit the elite's win-win model. Sometimes the pressure to conform forces these critics to water down their radical messages.

However, those who generate ideas that maintain the integrity of the current system are lauded as thought leaders worth listening to. Such individuals are paid handsomely through speaking engagements and book deals. Giridharadas states that society as a whole suffers whenever voices of change are silenced and branded as a bunch of losers.

Key Takeaway: The rich prefer a status quo where people learn to adapt to their problems.

Giridharadas contends that the wealthy don't like it when they are made to feel guilty for how they make their money. Therefore, they quickly embrace messages that focus on global awareness and social consciousness. Individuals like Andrew Zolli have tapped into this narrative by being paid to give solutions that don't change fundamental things.

After writing a book on resilience, Zolli began preaching a message that focused more on enduring current world problems instead of getting to their root causes. For example, instead of people complaining about climate change, they should learn to survive rising sea levels. Instead of fixing the foster care system, foster kids should be trained to be more psychologically resilient.

Such messages are hugely popular with the elite because they don't interfere with the status quo. Humanity is better off "rolling with the waves instead of trying to stop the ocean." The wealthy don't want to hear ideas that involve them losing the power they hold over the masses.

Key Takeaway: Critics are marginalized while thought leaders are embraced.

When it comes to thinking and generating ideas, two kinds of thinkers emerge. There are the public intellectuals, or critics, who are constantly agitating against systemic inequality. Critics tend to present their arguments via magazines and books. Then there are thought leaders who go easy on the plutocrats because they sponsor most of today's conferences. Thought leaders usually come up with ideas that promote the interests of entrepreneurs.

Critics are a dying breed while thought leaders are taking over the ideas industry. According to Giridharadas, there are three factors that explain why critics are declining:

- **Political polarization** – US politics has become so tribal that people only want to hear from those who confirm their opinions.

- **Loss of faith in institutions** – People don't trust the media, which is the primary platform of public intellectuals.

- **Rising inequality** – As more people try to find solutions to rising inequality, more billionaires are emerging to fund social ideas. Therefore, society seeks out individuals whose ideas will attract the wealthy.

Key Takeaway: Public intellectuals are often coerced to join the bandwagon of thought leaders.

Surveys show that potential critics are often enticed to abandon their harsh stance and join the elite. As the wealthy get richer, they start to seek more education. But instead of going to school, they decide to bring the teachers to them. The elites invite these critical thinkers to events such as TED, the Aspen Ideas Festival, and South by Southwest. It is very difficult to refuse such lucrative opportunities. Critics find themselves gradually toning down their ideas and unwittingly find themselves turning into thought leaders.

Giridharadas states that other factors have also forced public intellectuals to gravitate toward private interests. There are fewer academics receiving tenure on campuses. The publishing industry is also suffering major losses as people rely more on digital sources to learn new ideas. Private support is gaining influence, and unfortunately, these new patrons have specific taboos and tastes. Thinkers must compromise in order to stay relevant.

Key Takeaway: Critics go through three stages to transform into a thought leader.

Giridharadas contends that there are basic steps that define how a critic becomes a thought leader. The first step is to shift attention onto the victim rather than the perpetrator. Whenever a problem arises, your instinct is to look for a wrongdoer. However, this is a win-lose way of finding a solution because it triggers anger. By focusing on being empathetic toward the victim, you are able to provide a more constructive solution.

The second step is to turn political issues into personal ones. For you to become a thought leader, you must help people see systemic and collective problems as individual issues. For example, instead of talking about how racism has disenfranchised African Americans for centuries, you should focus on sagging pants as the problem. Thought leaders lead the public to think smaller instead of bigger.

The third step is to provide constructively actionable solutions. Critics are allowed to complain about problems. However, a thought leader must offer a list of potential solutions. The elite love it when a thinker provides uplifting ideas that give people hope, even if the solution never changes the underlying causes.

CHAPTER 5:
ARSONISTS MAKE THE BEST FIREFIGHTERS

Whenever a social problem arises, experts are usually assembled to think of the best solutions. These so-called experts are often consultants and advisers of large private corporations that know absolutely nothing about the issue at hand. To make matters worse, these problem solvers work for companies that contribute to many of the social ills that society currently faces.

According to Giridharadas, their perspective is often limited because they lack the local knowledge necessary to devise real solutions. However, corporations have found ways of edging out other key players when it comes to driving social change. This has led to short-sighted ideas that benefit the elite more than the common man.

Key Takeaway: The business world doesn't always have the best answers for social problems.

Giridharadas contends that some wealthy individuals aren't fully sold on the elitist win-win approach to solving society's problems. Men like George Soros are still funding social causes that aren't market-oriented. However, as social change begins to be dominated by the win-win model, even Soros' foundations have to rely on individuals with corporate expertise to help implement their agenda.

When Sean Hinton was hired by Soros to provide ideas on how to create a more inclusive economy in developing nations, he instinctively gathered a group of individuals who worked for private equity firms and multinational corporations. Instead of focusing on justice, equality, and the power structures that prevented them, the meeting veered in a different direction. The experts focused solely on the data and forgot about the people who would be affected by their decisions.

For example, when discussing how to enhance the farm supply chain in rural India, they talked about eliminating the intermediaries between the farmers and the consumers. However, they failed to consider whether the majority of these intermediaries are women. Eliminating their role would increase poverty. Furthermore, these intermediaries also ensured that the small villages along the way received fresh produce instead of relying on unhealthy processed foods.

Key Takeaway: Experts rely on market protocols instead of the people on the ground.

According to Giridharadas, the solutions that the business world comes up with ultimately fail because they don't rely on local knowledge. When you go to a foreign country, the best way to add value to the local community is by observing, listening, and learning from the local population. You hang back, connect with people, and avoid making any assumptions. This humble approach will help you generate the best solutions to local problems.

However, large corporations don't follow such an approach. Companies like McKinsey expect their consultants to swoop in with preconceived ideas and presumptions based on set protocols. These protocols are designed to generate facts and data that are totally unrelated to the people on the ground. You don't have to come up with the right answer. All you have to do is break down the problem into tiny pieces and use logic and facts to make an educated guess. Giridharadas argues that these market-based protocols create solutions that obscure the real problem.

Key Takeaway: Business protocols are touted as solutions, yet they are the cause of social ills.

Public problems are often expected to be solved by the civil society or government. However, corporations are using their business protocols to elbow out public servants. Even charity and civil rights organizations are placing business-minded people on their boards.

Giridharadas explains how some companies use protocols to fight for the oppressed. TechnoServe claims to be interested in "linking people to information, capital, and markets...to create lasting prosperity." According to them, people are poor because they lack linkages. Yet the truth is that poverty is a result of plunder, unfair labor practices, low wages, racism, etc. Such a limited view of social challenges seeks to elevate the elites as saviors instead of plunderers of resources.

How can corporations in the energy sector be expected to fight climate change when they are contributing to it? How can businesses create strategies for women's rights, yet their workplace policies don't include maternity leave or daycare? You cannot solve a problem using the same tools that caused it.

Key Takeaway: Globalization, optimization, and financialization have diminished the concept of shared value.

Shared value is an approach where a company achieves its business goals while also improving its relationship with the community. However, there are some increasingly popular business practices that are harming communities. The first is globalization. Giridharadas states that traditionally, businesses supported the local community by investing in public schools, buying local inputs, paying local taxes, and saving profits in the local bank. But with globalization, companies only care about investing wherever the best opportunities can be found. If the community doesn't create the right opportunities, the company leaves.

Optimization has also led to the loss of shared value. Companies now want to optimize every little process without examining the impact on the whole system. Thanks to optimization tools, employees are facing lower wages and inconsistent work schedules. Though businesses are becoming more productive, optimization is creating a divide between employers and employees.

Companies are today more concerned about shareholders and stock prices. This *financialization* phenomenon is great for short-term profits. However, it ultimately ruins the relationship between the company, the community, or its workers.

CHAPTER 6: GENEROSITY AND JUSTICE

If there is one thing that the rich hate to talk about, it is inequality and its causes. Giridharadas describes how the wealthy perceive philanthropy as a favor done to the poor. The rich have no problems grabbing all the resources and then giving some of their wealth away. But they resist any attempts to change the unjust economic system. The elites want to be inspired to give back, but they hate it when someone tells them to stop taking advantage of the system.

According to Giridharadas, Andrew Carnegie is responsible for setting the tone for this kind of giving that takes place today. However, this is not how philanthropy began in America. Giridharadas uses the example of Darren Walker, president of the Ford Foundation, to illustrate how some individuals are trying to dispel the Carnegie gospel and create a better way of helping the poor.

Key Takeaway: The topic of inequality is taboo among the rich.

When Darren Walker wrote a letter castigating the way the wealthy practiced their giving, the philanthropy world was shocked. In the letter, Walker sharply rebuked his comrades by exposing their unwillingness to tackle systemic inequality. Walker blamed the elites for perpetuating an unfair system that allows them to reap huge benefits at the expense of everyone else.

Giridharadas argues that the crisis of inequality is one topic that the rich never want to talk about. They would rather find ways of reducing poverty than reforming the systems that keep people poor. Walker received a lot of backlash from many plutocrats, with one of his friends telling him, "I just think you should stop ranting at inequality. It's a real turnoff."

Key Takeaway: Giving was founded on common associations, not big philanthropy.

According to historians, the American tradition of giving initially took the form of grants to government and public institutions that had legislative oversight. Sometime in the late 19th Century, there was a rapid increase in the gap between the rich and the poor, thanks to an increase in global trade. Due to immigration and disease outbreaks, the people formed voluntary fraternal associations to help each other financially. The rich supported the poor and built schools and hospitals.

But in the early 20th Century, tycoons like Carnegie and Rockefeller used their vast fortunes to create private charity foundations. The private entities were created simply to calm down the angry masses that hated the increase in inequality. Unlike the charity associations of the past, these new philanthropic entities were run by a handful of wealthy professionals and were self-governing.

Key Takeaway: Big philanthropy has always had critics and supporters.

Though foundations are extremely generous, Giridharadas contends that there are major criticisms to big philanthropy. The first is that the wealth being distributed is ill-gotten. Rockefeller is known to have held a tight monopoly over the oil industry and was extremely allergic to labor unions. Secondly, these large foundations use this ill-gotten wealth to gain influence in democratic societies.

On the other hand, men like Carnegie didn't see a problem with taking as much as you can from society, as long as you gave some back. Carnegie attacked his critics by stating that inequality is a normal part of human progress. He argued that the rich must be allowed to gain as much as possible because making money was a rare talent. Therefore, when the rich prosper, everyone benefits.

Key Takeaway: Minor improvements are meaningless without systemic changes.

Whenever a person of color manages to uplift themselves from poverty, the elite point to them as an example to be emulated by others. Yet the truth is that not everyone with a similar background can make it. As a black kid who was raised in poverty by a single mother, Darren Walker argues that he has seen the way the system is skewed against poor people. Even after rising to the top of the world of big philanthropy, he can still see how their efforts are failing to change the lives of the majority.

Walker explains how some of his family members are still struggling in life and how this makes him feel complicit. Though his life was transformed through charity, these interventions, no matter how large they are, cannot make a meaningful difference overall. Without changing the way the system works, a few like Walker may make it, but the vast majority will remain poor.

Key Takeaway: How the wealthy make their money is fundamental to solving inequality.

It is only through a deep investigation of the cultural practices and systems of doing business that inequality can be fought. One of the major stumbling blocks is the way the rich rationalize their actions. They believe in a false narrative where they have to preserve their wealth at all costs even if it means perpetuating economic injustices. Yet these injustices are the reasons why philanthropy is necessary in the first place.

The belief that inequality is a consequence of change is wrong because inequality is actually based on historical conditions. The racist, ethnic, and gender biases that have been fostered over centuries have created a society where some sections of the population are left so far behind they cannot take advantage of opportunities. The playing field needs to be leveled and society must talk about the way wealth is accumulated.

CHAPTER 7:
ALL THAT WORKS IN THE MODERN WORLD

The global elite has a single agenda for the world—to bring about a One World dream founded on borderlessness and free market economics. However, people are beginning to realize that this is a self-seeking agenda that is designed to make the wealthy even richer at the expense of the majority. Globalists are more loyal to each other than to the local communities they pretend to speak for.

Giridharadas describes how events such as the Clinton Global Initiative are merely talk-shops for globalists to bash democracy and anything that smells nationalistic. The wealthy fail to understand why the have-nots are filled with anger and resentment toward globalists. They believe that the world cannot run without them and people should just accept the skewed system as it is. But as more people begin to see through the façade of big philanthropy, a revolt is brewing all over the world.

Key Takeaway: The Clinton Global Initiative attracts opportunists, not philanthropists.

The Clinton Global Initiative is a much-celebrated forum that is regarded as one of the marquee events of UN week. Many people see it as a gathering of global philanthropists who are interested in helping communities all over the world. Giridharadas argues that forums such as this are actually talk-shops for globalists and elites who are only interested in finding fresh business opportunities. The fact that CGI is held the same week as the UN General Assembly meeting shows the level of contempt that the globalists have for world governments. Instead of helping governments directly, they create a parallel meeting that only benefits their bottom line.

Giridharadas explains how Bill Clinton uses his fame to raise money for worthy causes all over the world. However, he has shifted his focus away from supporting governments and now uses CGI to attract wealthy individuals and corporations. These billionaires aren't as much interested in raising funds to prevent HIV as they are in reaping huge profits from selling drugs to poor people. While others see poor people who need to be helped, globalists see business opportunities.

Key Takeaway: Private philanthropic events are for the lucky few.

When world leaders meet during the UN General Assembly, everyone recognizes the event as a public forum where public problems are discussed. However, the other side events that occur around the same time are mostly private forums where the elite meet to talk about solving public problems. Giridharadas describes how out of 64 events sponsored by private corporations, only eight are free. To attend the rest, you have to pay or receive a private invite.

This discrepancy reveals how the wealthy see their role in world affairs. Though the problems they are discussing in these forums are public in nature, the solution only lies in the hands of a few private citizens. By locking out the masses from contributing to solutions, the elite are saying that public problems are none of the public's business.

Key Takeaway: When the masses lose trust in the elite, a revolt is inevitable.

The majority of people all over the world are increasingly aware that the wealthy in society are only interested in serving their own interests. This has led to a rise in populist anger in society. The perception is that meetings such as CGI are forums where the wealthy protect their interests instead of making society better for the most marginalized groups. Giridharadas states that the elite are aware of and worried about this resentment. He describes how in early 2016, the world's elite met in Davos and laughed at the prospect of Donald Trump clinching the Republican nomination. They also ignored the signs that Britons would vote to exit the European Union.

These are indicators that the people are losing faith in the current system and are expressing their anger against the status quo. Yet the elite still wonder why they are hated so much. They fail to see that though the beliefs they cherish are good—open borders, market cures, etc.—the people want to have a greater say in how their problems are solved. Globalists only think of one big world but forget that the average person is struggling with local problems that require a local solution.

Key Takeaway: Globalists don't know how to deal with populist anger.

Giridharadas contends that the biggest threat to globalization isn't the nationalistic populists but the globalization cheerleaders themselves. The language that globalists use is insulting and alienating to the masses.

When Bill Clinton is asked about the rise in populist anger, he states that people feel excluded from the decision-making process. They feel like the government doesn't really care about their issues anymore. But when prodded for a solution, Clinton says that there needs to be a greater partnership between the private sector and government. In his opinion, the best way to quell populist anger against globalization is to increase the influence of elites in government. This shows that globalists are ignorant about what the majority really want.

EDITORIAL REVIEW

In his book *Winners Take All*, Anand Giridharadas argues that the world's elite are the reason why there is so much poverty and inequality all over the world. The fact that these wealthy individuals and corporations are major philanthropists doesn't mean they are interested in social change. Their aim is globalization—to create a world based on free-market economics and no borders. Everything they do and every penny they give is simply a way to gain a greater foothold in economies all over the world. In other words, the poor people they are claiming to help are simply a market to sell more of their goods.

These MarketWorlders, as Giridharadas calls them, only care about their bottom line. Some of the claims that the author makes may sound incredulous, but the fact that Giridharadas provides direct quotes from these individuals makes his assertions credible. For a long time now, people have accepted that the rich must help the poor. But the truth is that most people don't realize that they are poor because of their generous benefactors. The rich manipulate the system at the expense of the poor.

The book is packed with first-hand statements made by the elite. The fact that Giridharadas himself was part of the elite as a Henry Crown fellow at the Aspen Institute says a lot about his level of insider knowledge. In his interviews, he exposes how the wealthy view the rest of the world. Great men like Carnegie and Rockefeller believed that it is okay for them to abuse the system to get rich, just as long as they gave some of their wealth back. Globalists like Bill Clinton believe that its only private enterprises that can bring about real change, regardless of whether these corporations are the same ones polluting the environment and poisoning the water supply. The problem is that private corporations are having so much influence on social change that they are even threatening the democracies that the public dutifully votes for.

All is not lost, however. There are some few individuals who have risen to the top and have seen the light. The only problem is that they are not having an easy time convincing their fellow elites to tackle systemic inequality. The rich want to talk about poverty reduction and giving, not increasing wages, paying more taxes, or ending discrimination in the workplace.

Giridharadas does a good job of revealing how the elites think. Each chapter is packed with great insights and examples of corporations that do things that many would consider unjust. Some may find the information somewhat repetitive, but that is because the running theme throughout the book is consistent—inequality is perpetuated by the same elites who act as the world's biggest philanthropists.

At the same time, Giridharadas should have done a better job of providing meaningful solutions to this impasse. The wealthy are not going to change the system, so what now? The people are rising up in anger, as can be seen in the Brexit vote and presidential election of the populist Donald

Trump. The elites are worried that their MarketWorld values are being rejected. It's time for the world to take a fresh look and approach on how to fix the problem of inequality.

BACKGROUND ON AUTHOR

Anand Giridharadas is an author and journalist. He has published two other books, namely *"The True American: Murder and Mercy in Texas"* and *"India Calling: An Intimate Portrait of a Nation's Remaking."*

Born in Cleveland, Ohio in 1981 to Indian parents, Giridharadas attended Sidwell Friends High School. Afterward, he joined the University of Michigan and graduated with a degree in politics and history. At the age of 17, he began writing for the Washington Bureau of *The New York Times* newspaper.

He briefly worked with McKinsey & Company as a consultant in Mumbai. In 2005, he went to work as the Mumbai correspondent for *The New York Times*. When he came back to the United States in 2008, he became a columnist for the *Times*, authoring columns such as "Letter from America," "Admit One," and "Currents." He has also written business, arts, foreign, and travel pages for the *Times*, as well as for *The New Yorker* and *The Atlantic*.

Giridharadas currently works as an on-air political pundit for MSNBC and NBC News. He is also a visiting scholar at New York University's Arthur Carter Institute of Journalism. He has given numerous TED talks and is also a Henry Crown Fellow.

He currently lives with his wife Priya in Brooklyn New York. They have a son called Orion and a daughter named Zora.

TITLES BY ANAND GIRIDHARADAS

India Calling: An Intimate Portrait of a Nation's Remaking (2011)

The True American: Murder and Mercy in Texas (2014)

Winners Take All: The Elite Charade of Changing the World (2018)

END OF BOOK SUMMARY

*If you enjoyed this **ZIP Reads** publication, we encourage you to purchase <u>a copy of the original book</u>.*

We'd also love an honest review on Amazon.com!

44188465R00029

Made in the USA
Lexington, KY
08 July 2019